Power, Love, and a Sound Mind

How Three Simple Truths Changed My Life

DENISE R. NIXON

WESTBOW
PRESS®
A DIVISION OF THOMAS NELSON
& ZONDERVAN

Scripture taken from the New King James Version®. Copyright © 1982 by Thomas Nelson. Used by permission. All rights reserved.

WestBow Press books may be ordered through booksellers or by contacting:

WestBow Press
A Division of Thomas Nelson & Zondervan
1663 Liberty Drive
Bloomington, IN 47403
www.westbowpress.com
1 (866) 928-1240

ISBN: 978-1-9736-5076-8 (sc)
ISBN: 978-1-9736-5077-5 (e)

Print information available on the last page.

WestBow Press rev. date: 03/27/2019

CONTENTS

PREFACE

Are you questioning your purpose and your true passion in life? Maybe you have been wondering what else there is for you out there. Or maybe you know that you are not walking in your purpose, and you need to know that there are others out there who are in the same place. Or maybe you are like I was, struggling to meet a standard and expectation that you didn't even want for yourself. Other people's opinions and expectations play in your mind daily to become what they expect you to become. No matter what your questions are, I believe that you are moving closer to finding your true purpose because you are thinking about it and trying to figure it out. I must admit, there is no greater method of transparency (except prayer) than writing a book because it requires reflection, research, and exploration. I hope that you can reflect on your inner value and hopes because you are worth it.

I've received many great things thus far during my life – many accolades, compliments, degrees, certifications, licenses and awards. All things are to the glory of God. Each award shows what God can do through anyone. I am no different from anyone else. I claim the favor God gave me, and I will never be ashamed of that. I am sharing this book with you because I want to tell you that God will never give up on you, no matter how "messed up" you think you are. In my journey on this earth so far, I have discovered that God has placed worth in everyone. Unfortunately, we often look for value and worth in material things. This is what made me realize what is most important in life. No amount of money or material wealth can ever create a happy life. True happiness and peace can only be found in a relentless trust and journey toward God through Jesus Christ.

Sometimes, when you take something back to a store without a receipt, some stores tell you that they cannot give you a refund, but you can make an exchange for something of equal or greater value. Well, I made a great exchange – I exchanged a six-figure salary for purpose and peace that surpasses all understanding. I realize that wealth is not a sin, but we must keep our priorities in order. Finding purpose can lead us to victory and prosperity. The Bible says in Proverbs 18:16, "A man's gift makes room for him, and brings him before great men." The ability to be able to use the gifts God gave me to help others, to spend more time with myself and others, and to be available – is priceless. As a matter of fact, in this department store of life, what I brought to the counter to exchange does not begin to measure up to what I received. I am actually left owing on this exchange because what I received is worth so much more than what I gave. When we place God first, we can truly find our purpose and live the abundant life He called us to live. I found a deeper meaning to my life, realizing that it is not all about me. It is all about God. I am learning to stand on His promises.

Look at God – the price Jesus paid on the cross – we can never repay. But isn't this wonderful? God looks at all of us and says without hesitation, "You are worth it!" If you are reading this book and are looking for answers, I hope you find them, and I am sure that through life experiences and Godly counsel, you will. However, I am willing to share the simple truths revealed to me that I am still learning in this awesome master class taught by the Master Himself. His classes run year round, any time of day or night, free enrollment, no textbook fees. You can never be late, and there's always a seat – for you.

It does not take a long time to express my point, and for that reason, you will find that this book is not extremely long. These are my experiences in my walk and search for purpose, and I am sharing some of the Bible verses that I am meditating on as I reflect on my experiences. This book is not intended to take any scripture out of its purpose, meaning or context. I am still growing, walking and praying in God's presence. He has given me a peace that surpasses all understanding, and I hope that if you do not have peace, that you will find it through Him. And once you find that peace and purpose, there is no turning back.

If you find yourself in a hurry and want to dive right into the subject, check out Simple Truth #1 on how to keep your focus on what truly matters, and be sure to read the types of negative people you may encounter on your journey to purpose. Also, you can't skip Simple Truth #2 and the seven types of faiths. And Simple Truth #3 discusses how God is always available to you. I guess you may just have to read the whole book!

Here are the three simple truths that changed my life. May they be as powerful for you as they still are for me.

For God has not given us a spirit of fear, but of power and of love and of a sound mind.

II Timothy 1:7 (NKJV)

ACKNOWLEDGMENTS

I give honor and praise to my Lord and Savior, Jesus Christ, who died for my sins and made me whole. God is exactly who He says He is.

My heartfelt gratitude goes to my family for motivating and encouraging me to write this book and in my journey to finding my purpose in becoming an entrepreneur – my mother, Dorothy Nixon, my brother and his wife, Derek and Erin Nixon, and my brother and his wife, Arthur and Angelia Nixon. I am so proud of my niece, Jordan, and my nephews, Christopher and Seth.

My deep gratitude and gratefulness go to my church family, Grant Hill Missionary Baptist Church, for encouraging and strengthening my faith.

SIMPLE TRUTH #1

Keep Your Focus

B eing busy has become a status symbol in our culture.
I once heard someone say that he asked a friend how she was doing, and her comment was that she was just so busy. His response was, "So sorry to hear that." What a response! What does that mean? Well, I like that response now because I used to be that person who was so busy. We'll come back to the "so sorry to hear that" response in a minute. Let's focus on the "busyness" issue for a moment.

Our society values the idea of being busy, which seems to imply importance, significance, a reason for existing, value, and success. I always heard my friends say that being successful means having a well-paid job, lots of education, benefits, big titles, and work stability. Now, don't get me wrong, there is value in these things, but they cannot become how you define yourself. In addition, you have to realize that there is a cost to having these things. I have learned that the more of these things one has, the harder it is to keep focus on what really matters – not impossible, but harder. It becomes a challenge, especially when the path to getting these things becomes crowded with the busyness of work and daily life. But what does it really mean to be busy, and why do we insist on creating the perception that we are so busy?

The greeting, "How are you?" is now just a formality and not an actual invitation for you to share how you are really doing. Are we that busy? Or is it that we just don't really care how others are doing? Maybe it's not that we are too busy. Maybe we are too busy with ourselves.

WHY ARE YOU BUSY?

Have you ever wondered why you were so busy? What was it that you were doing that caused you to be so busy? While you were busy being busy, how much of what you were doing can you remember right now? I worked for over twenty years in the field of education. Over the course of those twenty-plus years, I was a school counselor, a school administrator, and a district administrator. I was busy earning degrees, going to school, and working – all of the things that I believed I was supposed to be achieving. It was an inspiring, wonderful, stressful, and unforgettable experience. In the last half of my career in education, I expanded to teaching online, which I still enjoy doing today. However, during that time, I also truly realized the concept of "busy."

I was introduced to the field of human resources about 12 years ago when I was promoted to the district level to recruit employees. Recruiting is one of my true passions that I would realize much later. However, as I worked and was promoted over the years into various positions of greater responsibility, I became busier. My job seemed to drift away from what I truly enjoyed, which was recruiting. I no longer had time to spend with family and friends or attend events because of my schedule. I could easily put in 12-14 hour workdays and continue working even after I left the office. On the weekends, I was so exhausted that I slept on Saturdays just to refuel for the same schedule the following week. This went on for about six years while I was working in upper-level positions. Even my health and energy levels began to reflect my "busy" lifestyle. The years began to pass quickly, being defined by the schedules of the school system. A new year didn't seem to begin in January – it seemed to always begin in August. Life plans and events were scheduled around the school activities and yearly events. Social circles became defined by my job, and I dare say that even I became defined by my job. This is not good. Who am I, and what have I become?

Two years before I made the decision to leave the job, I reflected on my purpose. Why am I busy? It seemed like a simple question – maybe the answer was simple, maybe it was just that my position required me to be busy. There were a lot of people to serve, and it had to be done effectively and efficiently. But then, I kept asking myself, "Why am I busy?" I had not asked myself this question for years. I seemed to enjoy my work. I really enjoyed working with the amazing people in the education field. But then, more questions about my purpose came to my mind. Am I really doing what I was placed here to do? Am I fulfilling my purpose? Is this how my schedule is supposed to look?

WHAT ARE YOU BUSY DOING?

This is the part of reflection that may seem easy to answer, but it may not be as easy as you think. The automatic answer to this question may be, "Well, I'm working and supporting my family," or maybe you might even say that you are busy getting things done for yourself and other family members. Sometimes we may try to define our jobs as the things that make us so busy. Can you look at yourself and say that you enjoy the busyness of your life? If you can, that is great, because that is also where I am now, but I haven't always been here. If you're not there, it's okay, but you have to ask yourself what you plan to do about it. Life is precious and fleeting. Many think that they have plenty of time to make hard decisions, but the fact is that we do not know how much time we have on this earth. Each day is truly a blessing. Make sure you value your time. Working and being busy do not always have to be about making a lot of money or climbing the "ladder" of success. It should be about making a positive difference and helping others. The best thing about climbing that kind of ladder of success is that we should not be climbing it alone. We should be bringing others with us.

The part of my job that I loved was interacting with people and helping them move into their ideal jobs. So my answer to the busy question was that I loved helping people. Then the question arose – What are you really busy doing? Now, that question was the hard one! My days generally lasted about 14 hours, and it was not unusual to see my car parked at the office well into the night. I began my paperwork at about 6:00 pm because my office would be filled with people until then. After the office cleared, I would do my paperwork and return most of my calls before leaving at about 8:00 pm or later. I was "so busy" that I often could not even return phone calls for days. Of course, when calls aren't returned, people feel ignored, and that is not a good way to do business. Everyone has value. Again, what was I busy doing?

During all this "busyness," I made the decision to move from my current residence and purchase a house that was closer to my mother's house. This was an exciting adventure because I decided that I wanted to have a house custom built. I selected an area that was about two miles from where my mother lives. It was a new housing development, so I could select the space where I wanted the house to be built, and I could select all of the items in the house such as countertops, flooring, tile, floor plan – everything. I prayed about it, and I just knew that this was God's plan. I worked with the real estate agent on the plans, and I placed my current house at the time on the market for sale. Now, it was critical that my current house was sold before I could purchase the new one. I had faith that this was God's plan, so I moved forward. I was "busy" selecting carpet, countertops, the whole nine yards. I was "busy" making sure that all was taken care of for the house to be completed on time. I was "busy" preparing my current house for the market and preparing myself for the move.

Then, in the busyness of it all – my current house did not sell. Only one person even showed the slightest interest in viewing my house. I remember being frantic about hearing the potential buyer's remarks after they took a tour of my house, hoping that they would make an offer. I questioned the real estate agent about what comments they had about my house, hoping that they may have said something to imply that they were interested. I remember the comments just like they were made yesterday. The real estate agent said that the people who looked at my house described my house as "cool, clean and cute." What was that? What does that mean?? Is that what people say when they want to buy a house? Apparently not, because they didn't buy it. So, for the next several months, I waited on the phone to ring to tell me that my real estate agent found a buyer for my house. I never got that call.

What happened to God's will for me? I knew this was going to be my house that was being built. I drove past it weekly, watching it being built, watching the walls go up. I even saw the backyard being marked off for me. What was happening? I didn't understand this. God promised me this, right? So I kept being busy.

ARE YOU BUSY ABOUT GOD'S BUSINESS?

Eventually, the time came for the housing paperwork to be finalized and a closing date to be set. My current house had not sold, and I could not afford to maintain two houses. So, making one of the most powerful prayers that I have ever made, I asked God for His will, not mine, be done - and then, I left it alone. Yes, you are reading this correctly. I left it alone. I did all that I could, and then I left it alone. I called the bank, told them my dilemma, told the real estate agent, and left it alone. I could have possibly lost the new house along with the house I was living in. I could have lost a lot of money - but I left it alone.

During this time, I volunteered with a large church in the area that was serving Christmas dinner to the homeless and deserving people in need in their dining hall. My employer at the time promoted the event and was seeking volunteers. So I went, and I served countless plates of food to others. I never saw so many people who wanted to help, and I was moved by how many grateful people were there. There were volunteers there on Christmas day providing comfort to those in need. This is not to anyone's glory, especially not mine. This is to the glory of God, that He would allow me to witness these acts of love on Christmas Day. The fellowship with so many other people in the community was priceless. I left the event after all were fed, but I felt like I was the one who was truly fed, not by food, but by the Spirit. And guess what? I was so "busy" all that day. The same way I was busy at work not accomplishing much, I was busy on this day accomplishing more than I imagined.

So, the busy I was with the job and the busy I was on Christmas Day were different types of busy. I realized on that day that being busy about God's business is not being busy at all. It's being productive. And there is a difference. This difference is all about focus. Keep your focus on God.

Delight yourself also in the Lord, And He shall give you the desires of your heart.

Psalm 7:4 (NKJV)

In late December, the same month, I was released from the housing deal, I stayed in my current house, and another buyer eventually bought that house that I was building for myself. I decided to take my current house off of the market, work on making some improvements that would help the house sell, and wait on God.

Now, let me say a word about waiting. Waiting on God is not a passive activity. So, while I waited, I began painting my current house, removing outdated carpet, and fixing minor issues. I even contacted another real estate agent to come to my home to give me advice on what would sell my house so that when I was ready to sell, the house would be ready. The agent came to my house and gave me some great advice. I noticed that as she was leaving my house that day, it was pouring rain. I mean, really hard. I did not realize it at the time, but the rain would have a deeper meaning in my story.

BUSY IN AN INSTANT

I took the real estate agent's suggestions seriously and began to make improvements. A few weeks later, I found a business card of a painter in a flooring store, so I called the painter to come to my house and paint several rooms and remove wallpaper. I took a day off from work so that the painters could come by and paint the house. At the end of the day, I received a call from the same real estate agent who advised me on improvements to my home. She told me, "I'm going to sell your house." I laughed of course because I took this as her confidence in being able to sell it and her eagerness to list it. I told her that I wasn't quite ready to list it, and the painters were still working and had to come back the next day to finish. She called the painter by name and told me to tell him to be finished by early afternoon so that she could bring a buyer to look at my house. I was speechless, of course, because first of all, how did she know who was painting my house? Did I come in contact with a stalker? Was this the stalker real estate agent? What was going on?

Well, here's what happened. Being the well-known and phenomenal real estate agent that she was, she had many contacts in town that she worked with. That same day, she had taken a buyer to the neighborhood in which I lived. As the real estate agent passed by my house, she recognized the painters in my yard as some colleagues who had worked on houses for her in the past. The buyer also noticed my house and expressed interest, so the real estate agent showed the buyer photos from when my house had previously been on the market. One of the amazing things about this whole story is that the real estate agent had never mentioned the painter's name to me when I had met with her a few weeks earlier. I had randomly found his business card in a store.

The buyer came to look at my house the next day, and she made an offer, which I accepted. In an instant, my house sold. Now, of course, I had to find a house to buy. I found my new house in the same fashion as I sold my current house – in an instant.

My mother, who enjoys home decorating and online home tours, was assisting me in my search for a home. Shortly after the offer had been made on my current home, she called to tell me about a house about three minutes from her that she had found listed online as "rent-to-own." I drove over to the house and drove by it – it was perfect. So, I called the real estate agent, and she told me that the house was, in fact, a rental, and the current renter's lease was up. I asked her to set up a walk-through. The real estate agent suggested making a request for the sellers to replace the carpet. I looked around the house, and it was perfect. I made an offer, and it was accepted – with the exception of the carpet request, as the sellers planned to have the carpet cleaned. The closing was scheduled on the same date as the closing for the sale of my current house – one hour apart. However, God was not through yet. I had to take a walk-through of the new house I was purchasing before the closing. As I entered the house with the real estate agent and the home inspector, we were met almost at the door by water, flowing from the kitchen. Apparently, when the water was turned on in the house, a pipe burst and water flowed into the house during the weekend. The carpet in the living room and dining room was completely soaked! Water removal experts had to come in and ensure that there was no damage to the house. However, the carpet had to be removed. Amazingly, I did not have any hesitation in continuing with the purchase of this house. So, I had to quickly make a decision on flooring – I had the opportunity once again to make some choices about the kind of amenities that were to go into the house. Does that sound familiar? Anyway, laminate wood floors replaced the drenched carpet. Once again, water seemed to play a major role in the house purchase. Remember the heavy rain when the real estate agent came to assess my house? Well, this time the rain was inside the house. How about that?

On the day of closing, I met with the seller's real estate agent, and everything went as planned. The one question that stood out from the closing was from the seller's real estate agent. After we finished the paperwork, she asked me a strange question. She asked, "How did you know that the sellers wanted to sell the house? It wasn't on the market yet." I responded that my mother saw the house and that it was a rent-to-own offer. The seller's real estate agent looked puzzled and said that there was no ad like that out there. To this day, I firmly believe that God is also in the real estate business!

By the way, on the day of closing, when I moved to my new house – it rained. Also, the month I moved into my new house was exactly nine months after I asked God for His will, not mine, to be done. It took nine months for the vision to be birthed. It's not our time that matters, it's God's timing. He is not on the same time system that we are, and thank goodness for that. Sometimes, we lose focus, just as I had done. I still struggle with keeping my focus, but the one simple truth that I learned through these experiences is that, even if we lose our focus, God is still waiting and ready to pick us up. Keep your focus on God at all times.

And let us not grow weary while doing good, for in due season we shall reap if we do not lose heart. Galatians 6:9 (NKJV)

WHAT IS YOUR WHY?

When I was working on my former job, it seemed like my phone never stopped ringing. Even if the caller was asking about something that was not my department, I would make sure that the caller's concerns were addressed. I tried to always have a can-do attitude and to be a helper in all situations. Unfortunately, this led to many late nights and long working weekends. When you don't draw lines between your business and your personal life, you can become stressed and burned out. I remember realizing how extreme my lack of organizing my schedule had become when I would quickly take a restroom break at work only to be met by people looking for me in the restroom – "Hey, Dr. Nixon, are you in there?" Then it graduated to them finding out I was in the restroom and then proceeding to wait outside of the door for me to come out. I don't blame anyone for those situations – except myself. I created the environment for people to do that. How? I was always available, beginning early in the morning all the way through the evening. And I often responded whenever there was a problem or a need to be addressed instead of delegating it to someone else who could do it. This may not necessarily be a bad thing, but when you do not delegate appropriate channels, and when you have the attitude that in order for it to be done right, then do it yourself, then these kinds of situations may happen. This was another form of "too busyness" that I was experiencing.

When I decided to leave my job, I knew that I was taking a risk to pursue my purpose. I also knew that I may not see instant success in my journey, and I may not have a lot of support from my colleagues. However, I knew that God was with me, and that in due season His vision would come to pass. God was preparing me for the next season of my life, and I had to decide if I was going to run toward it or away from it. You can spend your whole career somewhere, working and helping, and it can all end in an instant. However, you cannot confuse your work with service. Service is what you provide for the greater good, to help someone move forward, and to help the company accomplish its mission and vision. We cannot confuse service by thinking that anyone owes us anything. That's when bitterness sets in. When I look back on this time, I realize that God makes us uncomfortable so that we can change, or maybe even leave, the situation.

> *My brethren, count it all joy when you fall into various trials, knowing that the testing of your faith produces patience. But let patience have its perfect work, that you may be perfect and complete, lacking nothing. James 1:2-4 (NKJV)*

But when He has a plan for you, follow it. I wondered why God was bringing me through this uncomfortable time, but I know it was to encourage others and to let people know that where one door closes, He has a whole house on the horizon (not just a window!).

I made the decision to leave my comfortable, six-figure salary job to pursue my purpose. Many people probably thought I was crazy, or maybe they thought I was running away from the spotlight or the pressure of scrutiny. None of these things were my reality. Instead, my hard reality was that my purpose in that position had run its course – and God was, in effect, showing me the door. However, it was a door that would lead to an amazing journey on which I am still traveling - and will never look back from.

I am grateful for the time I dedicated in service to the community, and it provided me with a foundation for helping others. I met so many people and made so many connections during my career. Now that God has brought a season of change to my life, I have embraced it running and rejoicing. Open your mind to new things, and let God handle the rest. All of these experiences, however, led to me discovering my purpose. So, for all these things, believe it or not, I am grateful, and here's why - when we get comfortable, we get complacent, and complacency is the blocker of creativity, passion, and performance. These situations helped me to realize my "why." I wanted to help people, but I wanted to be productive instead of busy.

Remember earlier I said that I would come back to the comment about being sorry to hear that someone is busy? Well, I didn't understand that comment before, but I understand it now. So now, when I hear people say that they are so busy, my response is also, "I'm sorry to hear that." I understand this now because being busy is not the same as being productive. So maybe when you ask me how I am doing, I will say, "I am so productive today, I can hardly stand it!"

Finding your purpose may not happen overnight, and your purpose may change throughout your life. Maybe your purpose was to be a great student in school, then to be a great parent, and then to manage your family. Or maybe your purpose began as working in the medical field for a while, and then you became a teacher to touch the lives of children. No matter what your purpose is, you owe it to yourself to find out what it is. Trust me, you will not feel that true sense of satisfaction and peace until you find your purpose and start walking in it.

ARE YOU BUSY NOW?

We often hear people describe their plan as their vision. I believe it is because we have to keep our focus on what we are doing in order to achieve our goals. Losing sight of your purpose can have you feeling lost and empty. You can have material wealth and lots of friends and family, but without the foundation of God, you will not feel like you are making a difference. I want to share with you a few things that I learned in my journey to finding my purpose. One of the most important things I learned was keeping my focus. What does this mean? It means staying focused on what really matters. I realized that a six-figure income could not begin to give me the peace that God has given me. Now, making a lot of money is not a bad thing, but if it interferes with your peace, then it may not be right for you at that time. We have to learn to count the costs of things in our lives. At that time in my life, the cost was too great, and what I was losing was my peace and my focus. I know that He gave me my focus – for that (and more), I am eternally grateful. He has prepared me to be able to handle now what I could not handle then. And I no longer have to give up my peace for financial stability. God can handle that, too.

> *You will keep him in perfect peace, whose mind is stayed on*
> *You, because he trusts in You. Isaiah 26:3 (NKJV)*

HOW TO KEEP YOUR FOCUS

Keeping your focus to find your purpose means being productive instead of just being busy. Inside of this simple truth, Keeping Your Focus, I discovered a few essential thoughts.

Essential Thought #1: Eliminate Negativity
while Embracing Positivity

Eliminating negativity is one of those things that is easier said than done. Before I left my job with the school system, I started my human resources consulting company called OneCore Workforce Solutions, LLC, where I assist businesses with designing training programs, recruiting employees, and other human resources services. I record monthly podcasts on my computer with a special microphone and something called a pop filter. I learned that a pop filter decreases popping noises and air hitting the microphone while speaking. It gives a better sound quality and does not emphasize the sounds of letters like "s" and "t" and others that may be more pronounced when using a microphone alone. Much like podcasting, in order to find your purpose, you have to develop your own pop filter. Not only do you have to watch what comes out of your mouth when speaking, but you must be careful what you allow into your mind and your spirit. Now, this is no easy task, because it may mean that you have to change some of your friends and associates, what you watch on TV, and what you listen to. You may have to change your habits, what you eat, and what you drink. For me, it meant more positive input, like sermons, positive friends, time with family, and it meant separation from some things which were not negative but had to be removed in order for God to do His will. For me, that meant some other things, including, eventually, my job. This choice is not for everyone, so you have to be in tune with God so that you are led to do what He wants you to do.

Achieving your purpose can be painful. My job was not negative because I interacted with so many great people. But my season was over, and God had another purpose for me. How do I know this? He began working on me two years before I left my job. When I discovered my purpose, I knew I had to find a way to make it a reality. I love to recruit and help people find their purpose in work, so I researched how to become an independent recruiter. I hired a business coach, and I began saving money and paying down bills so that I could transition into a new career when God said it was time. And sure enough, He led me to leave my job, and I have never looked back.

Now, let's talk about the negativity you must separate from. When you decide to walk in your purpose, not everyone is going to support you. There will be those who do not appreciate or recognize your journey, and it is important that you do not get angry and internalize their efforts to distract you. They are only distractions that will slow you down if you allow them. You may even lose friends, as some people only associate with you because of your job. I have found that everyone that I needed on my journey was revealed to me early on. Unfortunately, you will have to deal with negative people while finding your purpose. When you encounter them, do not let them affect your mindset or your goals. I encountered many negative people and am still encountering them today. However, God has empowered me to deal with them. I like to refer to the negative people as Purpose Boosters because they motivated me to move even faster toward my purpose. Here are some of the negative people, or Purpose Boosters, that you may encounter on your journey to purpose:

> **Purpose Booster #1**. The people who will no longer want to associate with you because you made your decision. That's okay, let them go. If you try to keep them around, they will only get in your way.

> **Purpose Booster #2**. The people who called you all the time because they needed something from you. They will stop calling. That's okay because they were only using you anyway. You should have more free time now. Read your Bible, you've got more time.

> **Purpose Booster #3**. The people who used your name because you were in a certain position who you didn't even really know anyway will act like they don't know you. That's okay, you don't even know them anyway, so you won't miss them.

> **Purpose Booster #4**. The people who talk about you because they can't understand why you left your job or made some other decision to walk in your purpose. They may even accuse you falsely, spread

rumors about you, ask you silly questions and try to tell you about negative situations and the rumors that are floating around. Avoid them – they will only get on your nerves and interfere with your relationship with God. They are one of the reasons that voicemail was created.

Purpose Booster #5. The people who avoid you now because you can't help them with their plans due to your new purpose. They are too needy and will deplete your productivity – let them continue to avoid you.

Purpose Booster #6. The people who will pretend to be interested in what you are doing but only care because they want to see how it will benefit them in some way. Remember, iron sharpens iron. You can't improve if you insist on surrounding yourself with people who do not have your best interests at heart. They are the reason that there are "power off" and "block caller" options on your cell phone.

Purpose Booster #7. The people who try to place their ideas for your purpose on you. You know, the ones who tell you what they thought you would be doing instead of what you know God called you to do. They may mean well (or maybe not), but stay in prayer and focus on what God's purpose is for you, not what people say they think your purpose is.

These are the Purpose Boosters that I encountered in my walk for purpose. The important thing to remember is that you cannot be angry with people who fit into one of these categories. God is elevating you to your purpose. You have to forgive so that your true purpose can be realized. You cannot profit from bitterness, anger, and resentment. You cannot be energized by revenge. It will deplete your resources and block your blessings. Trust me, I know. Pray for them and with them. Confess, forgive, and let it go. It will invigorate your spirit and renew your mind, allowing you to prosper and walk in your purpose.

> *Therefore, as the elect of God, holy and beloved, put on tender mercies, kindness, humility, meekness, longsuffering; bearing with one another, and forgiving one another, if anyone has a complaint against another; even as Christ forgave you, so you also must do.*
>
> *Colossians 3:12-13 (NKJV)*

You also have to surround yourself with people who will lift you up and inspire you. My mentor, who passed away in 2012, was the essence of a great leader and progressive thinker. He gave me some of the greatest advice that I ever received. In making my career decisions, there were two things that he left me with. First, with every career move I made, he told me two words – Be Ready. Notice that the words were not "Get Ready" but Be Ready. What is the difference? Why is it important in your walk and search for purpose? Remember, God does not operate on your time schedule. He does not appear like a rabbit out of a magician's hat when you want Him to appear. You have to be ready. If you want to be an attorney, then find a way to go to law school. You cannot become an attorney without preparation and education. If you want to open a hair salon, then find a way to get your education and your license. You do what you can do, and God will do what He always does – He makes a way.

Second, my mentor, before he passed away, was traveling late one evening by the office building where I worked, and he called me, asking me why I was still there. I tried to explain my late hours as an obligation to the job. He responded that I needed to go home. Then, several weeks later, after seeing me at work late again, he sent me this text: Balance – take care of yourself so you take care of the job. And that is all that the text said. Basically, he was telling me that I was doing no one any good if I was not taking care of myself. There was no value in depleting myself. His words played a major role in the leader I have become today. He was in effect telling me that I needed to find the true purpose in what I was doing in order to successfully accomplish the task. Quite honestly, what business people and contacts was I really going to reach at 8:00 pm? What work was I going to complete that could not be done during normal business hours? His kind words are what I pose to you, reading this book. Are you truly taking care of yourself so that you can take care of the job? Please don't let your response be that you are too busy to take care of yourself. Wrong answer! I know because I used to say that, too. Until one day, when I attended a meeting at my church, I passed out in the summertime heat during the meeting. My busyness caught up with me. And it could have taken me out if not kept in check. So I urge you to follow my mentor's advice. And I am going to add a reality twist to what he told me. Take care of yourself so that your job does not take you out. He was a great mentor, and his example of true leadership and courage will always strengthen my resolve to achieve my purpose.

I choose my mentors based on the kind of mentor he was to me. His advice was never selfish or self-promoting, always allowing me to discover the answers for myself. Surround yourself with people who will lift you and support you with positive thoughts and habits. They will be the wind beneath your wings.

Essential Thought #2: Embrace the Power of No – And Yes!

We always seem to hear about the power of no, saying no to people when they try to exhaust you with what they may need that you may not be able to provide. And yes, it is true - there are times when we have to say no. We cannot do everything. Sometimes, like me, we think that if you want it done right, then we have to do it ourselves. Well, as an entrepreneur, I have a new philosophy. If you want it done right, find the right people who can get it done, or invest in an automation system that will do it right for you. An example of this is in my current human resources business. I found a low-cost automation system that schedules interviews for me. In this way, I can save time during the day by screening resumes and sending requests to great candidates to interview with me. They select a time, and they receive confirmations to remind them of the appointments. This saves me so much time and effort, and it has really increased my business. I received positive feedback from candidates that they liked the system because it allowed them to cancel and reschedule on their own. The system is available 24 hours a day, so they can go online anytime and schedule an interview. Technology is amazing! But back to the power of no. One important way that I realized the power of no is in helping people. You have to realize, as I did, that you cannot solve every problem, you can't fix every hurt feeling, and you definitely can't make everybody happy. I think I just helped someone reading this book achieve a breakthrough with that statement! I felt it myself! You may be able to help someone along the way, and we should do what we can. But no, you can't pay everybody's bills. No, you can't be up 24 hours a day to answer every email immediately or respond to every text message as soon as it is sent. Answer them when it is reasonable. No, you can't be everything to everybody. No, you can't come to every function, and no, you can't make the sun shine or the rain fall. What's my point? You are not God, and you must say no to the people who try to make you their god.

How do people do this? They, maybe inadvertently, place unreasonable standards on you. They expect to see you at every function even though they themselves don't come to all of the events. They expect you to answer your phone whenever they call you, but when you call them, they are —you guessed it – too busy. It can be flattering at first thought that people hold you in such high regard. However, this can lead to burnout and frustration. I can imagine that there are many leaders, pastors, and executives that feel this way because people impose such high expectations on them. Sometimes, the expectations are so high that they cannot even attain the level of performance that is expected. As a result, they are left feeling like they have fallen short. Here is what we can say yes to – say yes to the expectations that God has for you.

> *Come to Me, all you who labor and are heavy laden, and I*
> *will give you rest. Take My yoke upon you and learn from*
> *Me, for I am gentle and lowly in heart, and you will find rest*
> *for your souls. For My yoke is easy and My burden is light.*
>
> *Matthew 11:28-30 (NKJV)*

Remember that God is always in charge – don't change bosses. Stop putting people in charge of your schedule and let God handle it. Believe me, when you work for Him, He has the best retirement policy and benefits package around. You can't beat God's employment options. When you say yes to what God has, you will be surprised as to what will no longer interest you or bother you. You will learn to put material wealth in its place and understand the real value and use of money. You will value what has been in front of you the whole time. People, time, even a cup of coffee is so much more valuable when you focus on God and view life through the lens of His word. I even began to realize the value and importance of healthier food and moderate exercise. I don't look for quick results or fads when it comes to improving my health. When you read the Word, it's like the Word becomes food for your spirit and thereby nourishes your entire being. Don't you ever wonder what it means when you hear ministers say to meditate on the Word? I would picture myself with eyes closed and trying to think of passages in the Bible to flow through my mind. But now I read my Bible and then just think about what the meaning is of what I just read. Then I read an interpretation of what I read for deeper understanding. And then I pray. God is the only One who can provide true meaning and understanding for His Word.

Before I began to walk in my purpose, I was overwhelmed, tired and exhausted from always working. I remember coming home late one evening and noticing that my house was in the same state that it was when I first bought it. You know, the unoccupied house scent, no sign of anyone living there, and no personal touches completed in many areas of the house. I looked around, and I asked myself, "What am I doing?" It was then that I asked God to take charge of my schedule. Now, when you ask God to do this, be ready because He is going to do just that, take charge. After I asked God to take charge of my schedule, I did not feel so pressured to always be at my desk at work. I began taking lunch breaks again at work, leaving work at more reasonable hours in the evenings, and drawing a line between work and personal life. I monitored my cell phone after hours less often. And then, I was able to focus more on God and less on other things. I still have a long way to go, but on this road trip, God is still driving. He doesn't need my faulty GPS. He's got this! Say no to foolishness, and say yes to all things that are of God. Keep your focus on Him, and He will provide all that you need.

Essential Thought #3: Who Do You Say I Am? Avoiding the Power of Perception

In the Gospel of Matthew, Chapter 16, Jesus asked the disciples who the people said that He was. They told Him the names of various people that others said He was. But then He asked, "Who do you say I am?" Peter answered and revealed that He was the Messiah, the Son of the Living God. This scripture is so amazing for so many reasons. But I want to focus on Jesus' question: Who do you say I am? Jesus started by asking the disciples about what people were saying. But He did not focus on that, He focused on what Peter said. The point is this: When you walk in your purpose, be prepared for people to call you what you are not. It may not necessarily be bad things that they think you are, you just can't let it bother you or deter you from your purpose. For example, our society may place judgment on people based on their marital status. I have never been married, and I will continue to walk in God's grace and mercy as a single person until or if God decides that there is a man out there that I should marry. However, you have to understand that everyone will not share your positivity. You have to embrace who God says you are in order to truly walk in your purpose. You can't run out and get married just because someone thinks you should. And you can't allow people to put you in a box because that is where they think you should be. People want to feel comfortable, but you were not placed on this earth for their comfort. You have a purpose, and God will guide you to find it if you trust Him.

I can remember being ten years old when my father died. My younger brother was 8, and my older brother was 14. My mother raised us by herself from that point, and she provided everything that we needed. One of the most powerful things that she did was to instill within all of us at an early age the importance of God and how He is first in our lives. God may allow things to happen in your life that are negative and cause you pain. But you have to remember that He is working it out for your good. You may not see it at first, but trust me, He is. And if He has a purpose for you, no matter how much you resist or how fast you run, you cannot outrun God's plan or His love for you. Remember Jonah?

> *Now the Lord had prepared a great fish to swallow Jonah.*
> *And Jonah was in the belly of the fish three days and three*
> *nights.*
>
> *Jonah 1:17 (NKJV)*

Jonah tried to run from God's will for Him. But God guided him back to the path that he was supposed to take.

> *Now the word of the Lord came to Jonah the second time,*
> *saying, "Arise, go to Nineveh, that great city, and preach to*
> *it the message that I tell you." So Jonah arose and went to*
> *Nineveh, according to the word of the Lord. Now Nineveh*
> *was an exceedingly great city, a three-day journey in extent.*
>
> *Jonah 3:1-3 (NKJV)*

So if I were you, I wouldn't test God. I'm not saying that He will send a whale after you, I'm just saying that His goodness and blessings will overtake you. So let Him drive. And to all the control-minded people – God doesn't need your GPS – He's got this. Be who God says you are, not who your co-workers, friends, and relatives say you are.

FINAL THOUGHTS ON KEEPING YOUR FOCUS

Ever since the age of nine or ten, I have worn glasses. I switch between contact lenses and glasses now, but the need for corrective lenses is still present. When I remove my glasses, I am limited to what I can see at a very close range, and even then I am not sure of what I am looking at. I have to take more time to figure out what I can see when I am not wearing my glasses. My glasses have to even remain in the same designated place so that I can find them when I wake up in the morning. Why am I telling you about my glasses? My faulty vision is not the point, but lack of focus is. Just like when I try to see without my glasses, when I try to view the world without God as the lens, the world seems crazy and out of control. I can't seem to make any sense out of anything that happens, and everything is a blurry mass of confusion. But when I look at the world through God's lens, I have perfect vision.

We must view and understand the world through the lens of God and His word. He gives us hope to trust in Him and believe without failing. No matter what you are going through, you must trust in God, knowing that even if things don't work out your way, that God's way is absolutely the best way. When we understand that God will not allow anything to destroy you, and He won't withhold any good thing from you, a peace that surpasses all understanding will come to you. You may be saying – but I'm not married yet! How can that be good? God is not through with you yet, if it is good for you, He will make it happen. But you may also say – I haven't gotten the job I want yet or the house I want – remember, He will allow whatever is good for you to happen. Remember His word:

*For the Lord God is a sun and shield; The Lord will give
grace and glory; No good thing will He withhold from those
who walk uprightly.*

Psalm 84:11 (NKJV)

Your desires will be shaped by Him when you delight yourself
in Him. Things that you once thought were important may not be
as important once you fully immerse in His grace. Try Him and see.
He will never fail you. Always remember what God says about you.
The Bible is full of His thoughts about you.

*For I know the thoughts that I think toward you, says the
Lord, thoughts of peace and not of evil, to give you a future
and a hope.*

Jeremiah 29:11 (NKJV)

SIMPLE TRUTH #2

Faith is a Choice

I truly believe that we can choose to have faith, and we can choose not to have faith. We always want to see a sign from God to know that we are walking in His calling, to know for sure that we have chosen the path He wants us to walk. But we can never really know, can we? Maybe that's where faith comes in.

MOVING INTO YOUR FAITH

I once heard someone say that instead of asking God to give us clarity in our daily walk, what we should be asking for is courage. Faith is believing without seeing, walking without sight. So if we ask for clarity in our prayers, are we asking to have less faith? Or are we trying to take the safe way out by having a definite sign to know that we are doing the right things and making the right decisions? I know that God communicates with us, so I believe He does send us confirmations in some way, shape or form to know that we are moving in the right direction. But we may not know it until we start walking. It's like driving to a destination in an unknown area, and you may not be sure if you are going in the right direction. But you proceed in faith, hoping to see some signs that you are on the right track. You won't know if you are going in the right direction unless you start moving. We have to stay in constant communication with God to make sure we don't miss those signs on the way to our destination. I remember that I was seeking a sign when I made the decision to leave my job. I felt deep within me that God was guiding me. And most importantly, I knew that no matter what choice I made, God would be with me. So what did I have to fear? God loves me so much that He can make my wrongs right. Just like a GPS will adjust if we take a wrong turn, I knew that if I took a wrong turn, God would recalibrate my footsteps to get me on the right track. How about that?? He has increased my faith.

So what is faith? Is it just doing without thinking? Speaking without meaning? No, faith is a choice. Faith is an action. Faith is a state of being which allows God to work. I still remember how I felt when I drove home the night I left my job. Even the music that began to play on my radio was anointed to encourage me – but that is another praise party topic for another book.

People think that in order to be a believer, you must be perfect and have it all together. No one has perfect faith. God didn't make us that way. All He wants is you, just as you are – broken, without faith, stuck in a rut, undecided, double minded, procrastinating, denying, lying, substance abuse filled, not perfect you – and me. That's all. So don't stress about being perfect. If anything, that will drive you away. To increase your faith, just come as you are, start praying and confess to God what you have done. He is the only one who can judge you. He can forgive what you've done, and He will heal your mind, spirit and life.

We have all heard eloquent prayers and long testimonies to God by people who we really see as being the faithful ones of God. These prayers uplift us and give us hope for every day, but let's be real. Some of us who are not that far down the road to living for God may feel a little intimidated. What if we can't pray like that? Does that mean our faith is not good enough? God doesn't judge us on how long or how eloquent our prayers are. I truly believe He listens to us even when we are not in prayer. Prayer is your communication with God. Don't be intimidated because you may not use the correct grammar all the time, or maybe your words are not long and eloquent. I believe God wants truth and sincerity. He wants you and me just as we are. So, to build your faith, just start talking to God in spirit and truth. Your faith will build daily if you continue to put in the bricks. Think of it like a house. Each day, take a brick and put it on the stack. A brick can be reading your Bible, praying and talking to God, asking Him for understanding, reading the Word about Jesus, trying to be more like Him or going to a church that spreads His word in truth and in liberty. If it is of bondage, then it is not of God.

> *Now the Lord is the Spirit; and where the Spirit of the Lord is, there is liberty.*
>
> *II Corinthians 3:17 (NKJV)*

So back to faith – I have observed seven types of faith so far. I know there are more, and these are not scientifically or otherwise proven. They are not levels or progressive from one to another. I think we gravitate between these often. These are the Denise-isms that I have discovered during my journey to discovering my purpose. So grab a cup of coffee and laugh and cry with me for a little while.

CHICKEN COOP FAITH

The first kind of faith that I discovered was Chicken Coop Faith. Chicken Coop Faith is the kind of faith that I think we all have at one time or another. It's the kind of faith that allows us to have a limited view of what God can really do in our lives. It's that faith that we have when we ask for the minimum, and we focus on the small picture instead of the larger picture. It exemplifies our small view of the world and how much we really need to grow.

We have all heard the stories of the chicken and the eagle. We look at a chicken that is limited in its ability to fly and reach great heights. We look at an eagle and its ability to soar above adversity and its enemies. We strive to become the eagle because we want to soar. In the book of Isaiah, we learned that if we wait on the Lord, we will renew our strength.

> *But those who wait on the Lord shall renew their strength;*
> *they shall mount up with wings like eagles, they shall run*
> *and not be weary, they shall walk and not faint.*

> *Isaiah 40:31 (NKJV)*

So we have been studying the eagle for a while. Yet, we still fall into the trap of Chicken Coop Faith.

Have you ever seen a chicken coop? For the readers who have never been in the country, let me give you a quick image. Even though I am a product of a military family, I have seen a chicken coop before, as my grandfather was a farmer. I have beautiful memories of the farm where he and my grandmother lived for many years. He built the farm himself, and he had many animals, including chickens. When we went to visit them, my brothers and I used to enjoy watching him with the chickens. I won't go into what he used to do when it was time for one of the chickens to become dinner – that's another topic. However, when we watched the chickens in the coop, I noticed that the coop was made of some type of wire material, so that the chickens can see outside, could possibly even roam outside of the coop if the door was open, and the chickens could be fed through the coop. However, the coop had a top on it which prevented them from being able to fly out or go too far. Some coops that I have seen are totally enclosed in a large area so that the chickens cannot leave the coop.

Do you have faith that allows you to think outside of the coop? Chicken Coop Faith is the mentality that we believe that God can only do what we allow Him to do in our lives. He can do only what we can see. When we ask Him for just enough money to pay our bills when He can do so much more. It's when we depend on Him only for what we think is hard, but the impossible things we don't ask for because we have labeled them as such. Imagine what things we could accomplish if we could move beyond the chicken coop! I have met so many talented people who came to me and made statements like, "Can you help me find a job? It only has to pay the minimum wage, I only need enough to pay my bills," or they ask for a job that they are overqualified for because they don't really feel like putting forth the effort to find a better job. Please release the Chicken Coop Faith! If only we would believe that we are what God told us we are.

When I was struggling to discover my purpose, I experienced Chicken Coop Faith. I thought that I was limited to where I was at the time. It wasn't until much later that I realized that not only could I expand my purpose outside of my career field, but also outside of the state and the country. One of the people who motivated and encouraged me to begin my business lives in England. If we release the boundaries we place on ourselves, we can achieve so much more. In order to find your purpose, you have to think beyond your environment and your situation. Seek wise counsel from Godly people and remain positive. Choose to soar with the eagles instead of being stuck in the coop with the chickens. Believe what God says and who He says you are.

SLOT MACHINE FAITH

The next type of faith is what I call Slot Machine Faith. This is the kind of faith that can be masked as superstitions or even good luck charms. Slot Machine Faith is when we as believers fall into rituals, traditions or habits in order to get what we want. We believe that God will bless us if we do something a certain way. Slot Machine Faith can happen when we attend an event expecting a particular minister to speak, and because it's not who we were expecting, we are going to leave because we can't get anything out of his/her sermons. Or even worse, if we cannot sit in the seat we like, we cannot enjoy the message either. No matter who is delivering the sermon, God's message must take root in our spirit.

Slot Machine Faith operates like this. Think about when we put money in a slot machine and we hope for the winning result. We often rely on God like He is some sort of slot machine - if we put in enough good deeds and prayers, then we will get the jackpot. If we put money in the machine and do not receive what we are expecting, then we move to another source of satisfaction. We must focus on our motives and our intentions. God is not always going to give us what we want, but He will always make sure we have what we need. When things happen that are bad in our eyes, they are not necessarily bad for us. It definitely does not feel good at the time, but it is for our good.

Many people are hurting and going through challenging times. They may be having health issues or family issues, or they may be experiencing financial difficulties. Regardless of what we are going through, we have to understand that faith is not seasonal or temporary. Faith builds when we experience hardships, pain and turmoil. How can you build patience if you do not experience challenges that test it? Building your faith every day causes you to be able to withstand the challenges when they come. God's word says that trials will come, but those with faith who trust in God will be standing after the storm.

> *Therefore whoever hears these sayings of Mine, and does them, I will liken him to a wise man who built his house on the rock: and the rain descended, the floods came, and the winds blew and beat on that house; and it did not fall, for it was founded on the rock.*
>
> *Matthew 7:24-25 (NKJV)*

My point is this – don't count out the bad, there is purpose in what He does. God is intentional. He doesn't work by accident, He works on purpose. Just as He works on purpose, we must be in purpose. Lean on Him, He'll never let you fall. God is not a slot machine. Remember, His grace is sufficient. You can never lose by putting your all in God. Even if life circumstances seem bad, it is for a purpose, and it will be for your good. Trust and believe.

HEARSAY FAITH

Hearsay Faith is the kind of faith that doesn't require much planning, preparation or study. Unfortunately, I think this may be the most popular kind of faith, and I was guilty of practicing this kind of faith on my journey. Hearsay Faith is the kind of faith where we base our beliefs on what we see, hear and observe in daily life instead of picking up the Bible and learning for ourselves. It's when we go to church on Sunday, listen to the pastor preach a great sermon, and go home and wait for next week's sermon instead of meditating on what we heard or putting to practice what we heard. Or, it's the kind of faith where we are in a conversation with our friends or co-workers and someone quotes the Bible, no one knows if the quote is correct or not, because no one bothers to go look it up. It sounded good, right? We don't have time to research the word, so we just go by what other people say and do. We heard that God can do miracles, but we don't want to trust Him to do it for us. We heard that the Lord is our shepherd, but we don't really want to investigate what that means. We put more effort into investigating gossip than we spend on investigating the promises God made to us.

Another part of Hearsay Faith that makes it so popular is that it causes us to just go along with the crowd when it comes to God. We will use our own judgment to assess who we think is religious or of high character, and we may decide to just do what they do. This, of course, can be dangerous, because if we make decisions based on what others are doing instead of reading and studying the word for ourselves, we can get into a lot of trouble. So, we can truly find our purpose by studying the word of God daily and eliminating the possibility of Hearsay Faith developing.

It seems like if we focus on building our faith, we may not have as many incidents of Hearsay Faith. Maybe we can have an overflow of faith. We can learn through the things that we experience in our lives, but we have to understand that God has ordained for these things to happen in our lives. We have to study the word and be intentional about putting God first in our lives. In this way, Hearsay Faith can be reinforced by the everlasting word of God.

FAST FOOD FAITH

I was going to call this one Convenient Faith or Drive-Thru Faith, but I think that Fast Food Faith is more fitting. Why do we eat fast food? There are a number of reasons. First, we may be hungry. Second, it's convenient, as there are countless fast food restaurants around. Third, it's fast. We don't want to wait, do we? We will pull out of the drive-thru line and leave if it takes more than five minutes to cook our chicken, and we know good and well that we would take even longer to cook chicken at home. So what is Fast Food Faith? This is the type of faith that we feel is enough. It can't take up too much of our time. We want to put it in a box (a take-out box), bring it out when we need it, and then put it away when we are otherwise occupied. We don't want it to take up too much of our time, because we are busy. Let us be able to put it on the shelf during the week so that we can do what we want to do, and then when we are ready, we will take the box off of the shelf. How about that?

This kind of faith may last for a while, but when the storms come, and the rain falls, and the winds blow, it just doesn't cut it. The amazing thing about this whole scenario is that God is standing right there, waiting on us to begin to tip over like we are going to fall, and He will have His arms outstretched, waiting for us. That image brings tears to my eyes, because I know how it feels to have this kind of faith. Even in my ignorance, God was right there waiting on me. He's waiting on you, too. But He is not waiting on you to get perfect, to learn how to cook gourmet meals instead of hitting the drive-thru. You see, the thing about Fast Food Faith that I like is that it at least exposes you to a little bit of the word. This is not a long-term solution. It is the beginning. You must make an effort to grow from this, because it is also easy to get stuck here. We feel good just going to church once a week. We feel good paying our tithes. These are good things, but when you immerse yourself in the word, you will begin to see that there is so much more.

I went to a fast food restaurant one day for a meal. I placed my order, and when I drove around to the window to pick up my order, the cashier said, "Hi, you don't owe anything for this order. The person in front of you paid for your meal." I was so overcome with gratitude and surprise. That's how God is. We will be rushing through life and squeezing Him in where we can, and then He just does something amazing for us. I believe that is His way of getting our attention. Fast Food Faith is convenient, but it should lead us to a deeper relationship with God. Try Him and see – He is much more addictive and satisfying than those french fries we keep going back for.

CAFETERIA FAITH

I have some great memories from my childhood of being in school, especially elementary school. My family moved to South Carolina during my elementary school years when my father retired from the Army. Like most kids, one of my favorite times of day (besides band class) was lunch time and recess, because that was our free time to play with our friends. The teacher would line us up, pass out our meal cards, and take us to the cafeteria. When we entered the kitchen area to get our meals, we would proceed through the line while the cafeteria workers would fix the food, place the food on the trays, pass it along the buffet style line, and then hand it to us at the end of the line, with food already prepared and placed on the tray. The only choice that the kids had was the type of milk that we wanted to drink.

This is the foundation of Cafeteria Faith. This is the kind of faith that knows and trusts that no matter what God has prepared in the kitchen, it will be for our good. Like the cafeteria food, whether it was what we wanted, or what we did not want, we received it. No matter what Chef God is cooking in the kitchen, Cafeteria Faith says that we receive it to the glory of God. One day, it may be pizza and fries, your favorite meal, Hallelujah! Another day, it may be a casserole surprise and lima beans – Oh no! But whatever it is, God cooked it, so it is good for us.

Like the kids in the cafeteria line, we must recognize that we are not in charge of the food that is placed on our plates. Sometimes we get things that we do not want in life. God allows all that happens, if this were not so, then He would not be God, because we know that He is the beginning and the ending, the alpha and the omega. He is all-powerful and Almighty. We don't serve a God that has things happen that are out of His control. They may be out of our control, but never out of His. Knowing this, we should rejoice because He is in charge. Here is what I learned from Cafeteria Faith:

1. In order to receive what God has for you, you have to get in the line to receive it. Just like the kids in the cafeteria line, you can't dictate what you want. What if what you want is not right for you? Only God knows what is best for you. But you can ask God for what you want, for the courage to receive whatever He delivers, and the power to deal with it according to His will, so that He can do a great work through you. But you have to have faith and get in line.

2. No matter what God serves, it will be for your good. When God is cooking in the kitchen, He is not preparing anything that is bad for you. We may not like it, we may even desire something else, but what better food can we receive than the meal that God has fixed for us? The vegetables may not taste great at the time to us, but the vitamins and minerals that nourish our bodies make us feel better and give us so much energy. The bills may not feel good, the relationship ending did not make you feel great, losing your job may not have made you happy, the health diagnosis may not have been what you wanted it to be – but God is still in the kitchen, and He has a recipe for anything and everything that you need.

3. God is not a short order cook – we don't dictate what we want and expect to get our precise orders all the time. I wouldn't even want that. If God gave me everything I asked for, I would be in a mess! But what we can do is be in communication with God, and allow Him to speak to us daily. This puts us in the mindset of wanting and asking only for those things which He has ordained for us. In this way, we can be in tune with what God is fixing in the kitchen so that no matter what He prepares, it is all good!

You see, developing a relationship with God allows us to change our mindset so that whatever happens, we can deal with it. Even during the times that we do not understand His decisions, we can go to Him in prayer and ask what we will.

When we get in sync with God, we will discover that whatever we need, God seems to have prepared a meal to address just that. You may come to the kitchen deficient in peace, and He has a Peace Casserole waiting for you. You may come to the kitchen with despair, and you find that He has prepared a Hope Sandwich for you with a side of Solution Fries. You may even come to the kitchen lonely and dejected, and God has made you a Comfort Salad along with Love Pudding for dessert. Okay, my food examples may be going a little overboard, but my point is this: no matter what you need, God's got it. There's a song we sing at my church that has been passed down through the generations. It is a song that says whatever you need, God's got it. He's got everything you need. Those words are so true. Nothing is too hard for God. And if you let Him cook, you will discover that He is the best Chef around.

RED SEA FAITH

In the Book of Exodus, Chapter 14 Moses led the children of Israel out of bondage and away from the Egyptians. They came to a point where they were trapped between the Red Sea and the Egyptians who were pursuing them. There appeared to be no answer in sight, no way to escape. They thought they were trapped. But God...

> *Then Moses stretched out his hand over the sea; and the Lord caused the sea to go back by a strong east wind all that night, and made the sea into dry land, and the waters were divided. So the children of Israel went into the midst of the sea on the dry ground, and the waters were a wall to them on their right hand and on their left.*
>
> *Exodus 14:21-22 (NKJV)*

Red Sea Faith is the kind of faith Moses had when he lifted his hands toward the Red Sea. I can imagine that he did not know what God was going to do, but he knew that God was going to do something amazing and outside of his imagination. Red Sea Faith is thinking outside of your realm of understanding. It is beyond knowing that whatever happens, it is for the good. It is knowing that God is going to bring you out **and** defeat your enemies. You don't even have to know or understand how He will do it. You just know that He will. Perhaps this is the simplest and the hardest kind of faith at the same time.

Ask small children about their parents, and most of them will tell you that their parents provide for them without understanding how. And they also know and trust that their parents will provide for them in the future. Of course, little children won't understand that the parents have to go to work, make money, put the money in the bank, go to the grocery store, buy the food, cook it, and then put it on the table. All that the little children know is that the parents are going to do it. Easy, but difficult logic. Sometimes we cannot accept what we don't see. If we don't see a way, we sometimes think that there is no way. But God already said in His word that He can and will handle it. The one important factor that we must understand about Red Sea Faith is that we must believe. When we don't believe, we are setting up the situation that it won't be done. Look at what Jesus experienced in his own hometown.

> *But Jesus said to them, "A prophet is not without honor*
> *except in his own country, among his own relatives, and in*
> *his own house." Now He could do no mighty work there,*
> *except that He laid His hands on a few sick people and*
> *healed them. And He marveled because of their unbelief.*
> *Then He went about the villages in a circuit, teaching.*
>
> *Mark 6:4-6 (NKJV)*

Meditate with me for a moment on the part of the scripture that says that Jesus could do no mighty work there, and that He marveled because of their unbelief. Jesus marveled at their unbelief. What are we blocking from our lives because of our unbelief? What mighty miracles have we missed because we said they could not be done? What purpose are we missing out on because we think we can't do it? We serve a God who parted the Red Sea. He can initiate any storm or event to part those waters – who is like the Lord? We believe this, but we don't believe that God can work a miracle in our lives? We can't focus on how He will do it. Just know that He can. And that is the beginning of Red Sea Faith.

HOPELESS FAITH

Hopeless Faith is the kind of faith that we have all had at one time or another, but we may not want to admit it. This is the faith that makes us think that God won't do something because we did not get what we wanted in the past. Maybe we believed for a great job, but we were passed over for that promotion. Or maybe we hoped for a spouse or a new car, but it just didn't happen. You know you have been living right and following God's commands, but you still didn't get what you wanted. It almost sounds like Slot Machine Faith, because on the surface it seems like we are wishing and praying for things, and when we don't receive them we don't understand. We may even get angry at God. But Hopeless Faith goes deeper. Hopeless Faith causes us to believe that it is because of our own unworthiness that we did not receive these things. It's the kind of faith that is very personal and deep, because it causes us to judge ourselves and even blame ourselves for our own bad circumstances. We give up on God, because we don't see Him in the way that we think we need to. When we need money, we want to see Him as a money provider instantly. When we don't see the money instantly, we lose faith and we think that God won't do it. Hopeless Faith causes us to miss God's blessings. God can provide the money, but we have to receive the message in how He will provide it. God may not have a pile of money sitting at your doorstep the next day, but He may provide you with the opportunity for a job. He may not place the money in your hands, or place a money tree in your backyard, but He may allow a circumstance to happen where you are able to cover your financial obligations. God gives us the materials to build the outcomes in our lives. We have to learn to overcome the obstacles to reach our blessings.

When God blesses us, it is because He is so good, not because we are. Even in our sinful circumstances, He can still bless us. We must understand that when good things do happen in our lives, it is because of His grace and not because we were so good. And when things don't go our way, it is not necessarily because of bad things we have done. Remember, God is intentional. He does everything for a reason, even if we do not understand it. Sometimes we overthink things. Maybe God allowed you to miss out on that job opportunity because He knew that when you began making more money that you would increase your debt and get into financial trouble. Hopeless Faith prevents us from seeing the big picture. The beautiful framework of your life that God has created for you can be blocked by giving up on Him. Increase your faith, and don't ever give up. He is able to do what you can never imagine.

SIMPLE TRUTH #3

God is Available

I won't say that this is the last truth that I learned, but it was probably one of the most touching truths that I am still learning today. While I was searching for my purpose, I couldn't find anyone locally who could identify with what I wanted to do. So God began showing me others who were in the industry that I was seeking. The career field was crowded with people who were doing what I was trying to do. I had to expand my focus beyond where I lived in order to see that my dream was, in fact, a reality. Even to this day, many people do not understand what I do. They could not see what I saw. This is why sometimes you cannot share your vision with everyone. And for this reason, God is available. I want to share a few of the ways that God was available for me while I searched for my purpose.

GOD IS A CONTAINER

God will be whoever you need Him to be. Just like water, when we pour water into a round container, it becomes round. It takes on the shape of its container. If you need encouragement, God is a counselor. If you need joy, God is a comedian. If you need peace,

God is the best life coach. When I was researching my consulting business, I found out how much I needed to accomplish in order to get the business running. I remember that the only time that I was able to get the legwork done for getting business licenses, state licenses, contracts, and other necessary items was during my lunch hour. So God became a scheduler. For about eight months, my lunch hour was spent driving around in my car through town running errands to set up my business. I often took a sandwich and coffee to my car and made phone calls in the parking lot of my job during my lunch hour. I remember that one of the hardest things was finding an attorney. I had called so many people and left messages with no returned calls. Until one evening, when I was heading home from work, my phone rang. When I answered, one of the attorneys that I had called returned my call, and I still remember what he said. "Hi Denise, I see that you are trying to get your business started. How can I help?" God suddenly became a phone operator! The attorney didn't know me; he was a successful attorney, but he took the time to help me. In addition to that, he even met me in the neighboring city with the required paperwork that I needed while he was attending a conference. He actually stepped out of his conference just to help me and show me where to take my completed paperwork. God became a traffic director! When God has a plan for you, He will place people in your path to help you. He will make sure that you accomplish the mission.

The other part of this concept of God being a Container is that He is watching to see how badly you want to walk in your purpose. How bad do you want it? I record podcasts in my consulting business, and one of the topics of my podcasts was just this statement. You can tell how badly someone really wants something. You have to invest the time and energy to make your dream work. I was speaking to someone who was looking for a job, and when I asked him about applying for jobs, he said that he was planning on doing it, but he needed to get his resume together. He asked for help to get the resume together, and I gladly told him to send me an overview of his work history along with his education and career goals, and we would take it from there. That was three years ago, and I still have not received his information. How bad do you want it? It is up to you, be persistent and intentional in finding your purpose, and God will see your efforts.

In my consulting business, it was crucial that I had some way to collect resumes for the businesses that I would be working with. My first thought was that an applicant tracking system to collect resumes was way too expensive for me, and I would have to find another way. So I tried to manage the resumes myself and keep them in folders on my computer, and then I thought that I could create a system on my computer to manually go through hundreds of resumes to sort and find candidates.

> *But when he saw that the wind was boisterous, he was afraid; and beginning to sink he cried out, saying, "Lord, save me!" And immediately Jesus stretched out His hand and caught him, and said to him, "O you of little faith, why did you doubt?" And when they got into the boat, the wind ceased.*
>
> *Matthew 14:30-31 (NKJV)*

Guilty and convicted! I doubted the Lord's power just like Peter did when he got out of the boat. I doubted that God could make a way for me to streamline my business. When I saw that the need increased for me to have a system for collecting resumes online, I looked at my budget. I realized that I needed this system more than I needed to have gourmet coffee drinks from coffee shops. So, my sacrifice was gourmet coffee for an applicant tracking system. And guess what? I still brew my own coffee at home, and I still have my applicant tracking system. And it is all to the glory of God. God is the best HR Consultant! And He provides a great cup of homemade coffee, too!

GOD IS A TITLE MANAGER

When I was younger, I wanted to be a social worker. Then, I wanted to be a guidance counselor, then an assistant principal, and so on. I also went back to school and earned several degrees. But guess what? None of these things matter unless you put God in them so that He can show you how and when to use them.

I have found that the only titles that matter are the ones that God gave us. In the Book of Joshua, God had a plan for Joshua. He told Joshua, "Only be strong and very courageous." (Joshua 1:7, NKJV) He was preparing Joshua for the plan He had for him. What is God telling you? Are you listening? Titles are what people value. People look at titles to assess your worth. Titles and degrees have their place and their value, but use them to the glory of God, and you will see how they can be used in your purpose.

One of the funny things about titles is that you will find, as I did, that other people will be quick to place a title on you. Often, the title others give you may not be what you would call yourself. As you are seeking your purpose, there will be times that people will try to put you in their title box, placing restrictions on your potential. However, there will be other times when people will put titles on you that you don't believe you can achieve. Those titles could be meant to challenge you to reach your potential. You have to stay in touch with God to make sure that you are following His path and not someone else's thoughts and perceptions of you.

Before I left my previous job, I was confronted with many people's opinions about what they saw me doing in future years. Many of them stated that they could always see me working there, never leaving, and retiring from there. Now, that is not a bad situation to be in, and many people admire those who stay their courses and retire from an organization after 30 or 40 years of service. That is certainly to be commended. However, if that is not my path, then I cannot find my purpose in that destiny. I also had some people come to me and say that they could see me being a public speaker or counselor. I have done those things, but that does not mean that I am able to do only those things. Don't let others limit the possibilities that God has for you. Many well-intentioned people have limited the purposes of others by putting a label on them that they thought they should have. And many people often limit themselves by following that label and becoming what others say they should be. When you develop a relationship with God, He has a way of communicating directly to your spirit so that you know through faith that He is going to lead you to your purpose. Trust and believe, and He will reveal these things to you.

> *Trust in the Lord with all your heart, and lean not on your*
> *own understanding; In all your ways acknowledge Him,*
> *And He shall direct your paths.*
>
> *Proverbs 3:5-6 (NKJV)*

GOD IS AN EQUALIZER

This is a difficult section to write, because personally, I have a bit of a tough time releasing things to God. I mean, when you have been betrayed or hurt by someone you never thought would betray you, or if someone does something to make you really angry, you kind of have the impulse to get them back. Now, I hope you all are not leaving me out here hanging by making this statement. But for the sake of transparency and encouragement, I want to share my experiences.

Sometimes, people make bad decisions. And sometimes, you can be involved in situations where you find out the true intentions of people, and their intentions may not have your best interests at heart. I have a friend who shared with me that he always gets people back when they make him angry. While I was a little concerned about his comment, he was only being honest. You must admit, sometimes it may appear like getting people back is the right thing to do. God has allowed me to retaliate in the past against people who have made me angry. It felt like the right thing to do temporarily. Isn't that what society teaches us, to appear strong and not to back down? Aren't we supposed to hold a position of power at all times? You know what we call it – setting them straight, putting them in their place, or whatever terminology you may call it. Well, guess what? When I exercised this principle of getting people back, it didn't even last or make a difference. The negative behavior of the offending party continued, or even if it stopped, there was tension and more anger.

> *So then, my beloved brethren, let every man be swift to hear, slow to speak, slow to wrath; for the wrath of man does not produce the righteousness of God.*
>
> *James 1:19-20 (NKJV)*

That's when I learned the important principle of God being an equalizer. God will make it right all the time. You see, we have to remember that we all make mistakes. And I would not want people always getting me back. And I also would not want God to have to deal with me because I am following my selfish desire to win and be on top by getting people back. It is so much harder to refrain from revenge because we are reacting to hurt feelings or trampled pride. Often, the consequences of not retaliating make us want to retaliate. What I mean is, people will view you as weak, and they will make statements like, "You are so humble, but that's not me. I would have fixed them." These statements are often made in an effort to push you into doing what they may or may not have even done. People may often try to quote the Bible by using the phrase "an eye for an eye" or some other derivative of their understanding of the Bible. You have to stand strong in the faith and realize that what they say does not matter. When you stand before God, will they be there to defend your actions? More importantly, would you want them anywhere around you then?? Think for yourself, and pray for yourself. Read the word for yourself, and meditate on it for yourself. Get understanding, and desire His presence.

> *Get wisdom! Get understanding! Do not forget, nor turn away from the words of my mouth. Proverbs 4:5 (NKJV)*

There will be a cost to allowing God to handle situations in your life. People may take advantage of your kindness, viewing you as a pushover, or they may call you humble, or too nice, or they may even be rude to you. Speak up for yourself, but when it comes to retaliation to get people back, I have learned that there is no sweeter experience than allowing God to be God by letting Him handle those who have done us wrong. We cannot expect God to handle our offenders the way we would, or to ask God to do harm or bring negativity to our enemies. Remember, He loves us all, and you are not perfect, either. We all have sinned and fallen short. God knows how to handle it, so let Him drive and stop trying to take back the steering wheel.

Whenever someone does wrong against you, God sees it. And when we decide to get people back, then God may let us do it. But we cannot expect Him to endorse our foolishness. When people do wrong to us, God may be trying to teach us an important lesson in the experience. And I now know from personal experience that when God handles it, it is so sweet. Sometimes we may see the results of what happens, and sometimes we may not. But when you let God handle it, you give Him the opportunity to elevate and uplift you in the process.

GOD IS GOD

This is probably one of the most memorable lessons that I am learning. God is God. It may sound like a simple statement, but it is so profound. Only God can be God, no one else, including you and me. Let me give you an example of what I mean.

A colleague of mine called me one day, and she left a voicemail stating that she urgently needed to speak with me. About an hour later, I was able to retrieve my messages, and I listened to her message. Another person called me before I could call my colleague back. She called about three more times within the next hour or so. When I finally was able to call her back, her situation was not urgent at all. In fact, I can barely recall exactly why she was calling me. Now, I am not saying that this was not important. However, the world should not stop if I cannot return a call within someone else's specified time period. Sometimes, we allow others to become a god to us when there really is only one God. We cannot allow others to make us their god. I was one of those people who thought that I had to please everyone, and that everyone had to be happy when they left my office. One of the most profound lessons that I learned was that I was not put here to make people happy. Once you embrace this thought, you will be released from captivity. People are going to dislike you even if you buy flowers, candy, dinners, and anything else for them. Some people are just not that into you. Accept it and move on so that you can find your purpose.

Sometimes, people will make you believe that your job could not function if you were not the one performing in that role. They will compliment you and elevate you to try to convince you that you accomplished great things on your own. I once had someone who was very kind to compliment me, and I told them, "Glory to God, thank you." They seemed to almost get angry and they replied that, "The Lord chose you to accomplish things, so you should take credit and be proud of those blessings." I couldn't believe that this seemingly well-intentioned person was ready to have a debate on taking credit and giving glory. So I responded, with a smile, and told them, "Well, you are right, then on behalf of my Lord and Savior Jesus Christ, thank you." Speechless, the person just stared at me. **Never get to the point in your life that you begin to think that you are responsible for your talents and achievements.** That is a dangerous place to be in, and I will not allow people to try to put me there. People can try to make us their god, but we have to realize from whom our blessings flow.

While allowing people to make you their god is dangerous, there is another equally dangerous situation that you must be aware of. Let me illustrate this one with another story. When I left my job, there were a few people who constantly reached out to me to keep in touch and see how I was doing. Initially, this was okay and quite touching. However, the conversations began to lapse into less of a concern tone and more of a victim mentality mode. I began hearing questions and statements like, "Are you okay?" and "It's going to be okay." What were they talking about?? Then, I figured out that for some reason, they could not comprehend why I would leave my job, nor did they want to hear about why I left my job, so they began to think that I was in some state of hysteria or confusion. By the way, if you have been reading this book at least from the middle of Truth # 1, then you know that they can be classified as the 4ᵗʰ category of negative people (Purpose Boosters) that you may encounter when seeking your purpose. Once again, you cannot get angry at people, just stay focused on your purpose. You cannot allow people to make you their victim or their god. You have to be who God called you to be, no matter what people may say.

WALKING IN YOUR PURPOSE

Did you know that it may not always be comfortable walking in your purpose? Sometimes that may be when you know for sure that you have found your purpose. You have to be bold enough to know that God will take care of you, no matter what you are going through or what you must endure to find your purpose. People may talk about you, or they may support you. It really doesn't matter. What matters is that God has His hands on you, and He will never let you fall. It may not be easy to ignore criticism, and you may even have doubts as well. But the way that I knew that I found my purpose was when it seemed like God just kept sending me ideas for my business, and the clients began to come. I realized that if I put the work in, God would do the rest. He has, and He still is. He will bring the right people around you who are meant to help you walk in your purpose. If they are not with you, then they were not meant to be with you. Don't ever look back.

> *They went out from us, but they were not of us; for if they had been of us, they would no doubt have continued with us: but they went out, that they might be made manifest that they were not all of us.*
>
> *I John 2:19 (NKJV)*

The three simple truths that I learned that are presented in this book each have significance in my story, but collectively they have empowered me to walk in my purpose. You see, each of the truths embodies a promise that God made to all of us. *For God has not given us a spirit of fear, but of power and of love and of a sound mind. II Timothy 1:7 (NKJV)* I experienced the **Power** God gave me through the experiences that I shared in Simple Truth # 2 – Faith is a Choice. We have power through our faith. With faith, we can move mountains. Your mountain may be fear, doubt, insecurity, anything. Whatever it is, God has empowered us to conquer it as long as we place Him first. I experienced the **Love** of God through the experiences that I shared in Simple Truth # 3 – God is Available. I found out that He loves us so much that He will become whatever we need Him to be in our lives. He has us covered, even in our wrongdoing, providing correction and support. I truly have experienced a **Sound Mind** through the experiences I shared in Simple Truth # 1 – Keep Your Focus. He has given me a peace that surpasses all understanding. I have no reason or desire to look back.

Finally, remember that in all things, God is in charge. One of the Bible verses that empowered me was Philippians 4:13. Through my experiences in finding my purpose, I realized that I had to include the previous two verses in that passage.

> *Not that I speak in regard to need, for I have learned in whatever state I am, to be content. I know how to be abased, and I know how to abound. Everywhere and in all things I have learned both to be full and to be hungry, both to abound and to suffer need. I can do all things through Christ who strengthens me.*
>
> *Philippians 4:11-13 (NKJV)*

My prayer for you is that you not only find and walk in your purpose, but that you also have the **bold faith** to allow God to take the limits off that you have placed on your life and live to His glory, so that others may see His light in you. Be blessed always!

BIBLIOGRAPHY

Printed in the United States
By Bookmasters